CHINESE GODS
AND MYTHS

CHINESE GODS
AND MYTHS

CHARTWELL
BOOKS, INC.

Published by Chartwell Books
A Division of Book Sales Inc.
114 Northfield Avenue
Edison, New Jersey 08837
USA

ISBN 0-7858-1078-1

This book is produced by
Quantum Books Ltd
6 Blundell Street
London N7 9BH

Project Manager: Rebecca Kingsley
Project Editor: Judith Millidge
Designer: Wayne Humphries

The material in this publication previously appeared in
*The Atlas of Civilisation, the Atlas of Languages, The Book
Of the Sun, Chinese Brush Painting, Oriental Mythology*

QUMKG&M
Set in Times
Reproduced in Singapore by Eray Scan
Printed in Singapore by Star Standard Industries (Pte) Ltd

CONTENTS

THE ROOTS
OF RELIGION

The Chinese people have never demanded a clear separation of the worlds of myth and reality – indeed, they are so closely bound up that it is hard to say where one begins and the other ends. Historical figures are made into gods and myths are recounted as history. The early Chinese believed that the world was ruled by a succession of 12 divine emperors after the creation, and each of these was regarded as a god who ruled for 18,000 years. Ancestor worship was also a significant part of ancient Chinese ritual and remains a critical aspect of Chinese faith today. Despite its early trading links with the outside world, principally along the Silk Route, Chinese thought and culture were not significantly influenced by other civilizations, and they have remained self-sufficient ever since.

Opposite: The Temple of Heaven in Peking, where the emperor conducted the annual sacrifice to heaven and led prayers for a good harvest.

Below: A 17th-century Ming bronze of Laozi, the founder of Taoism. He is shown riding a water buffalo which carried him away from China to the west.

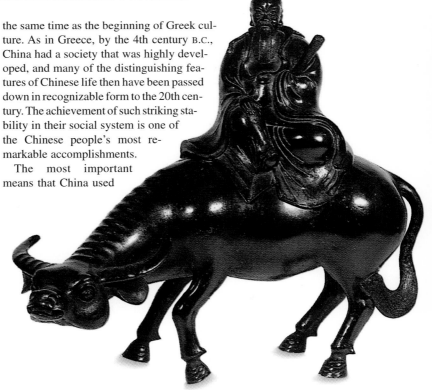

Confusing though the tendency to intertwine fact and fantasy may be for the westerner, it indicates the power and importance of "mythology" in the Chinese tradition. Even in the days of revolutionary China, the same processes could be seen at work: Chairman Mao, in the heyday of the Cultural Revolution (1968–78), was seen as an all-powerful god responsible for all good things that happened. When an airline hostess could offer the explanation that "there is no need to wear a safety belt, because Mao, the Great Helmsman, is in charge," the feeling is conveyed that superhuman characters with fantastic powers, like those that inhabited the ancient texts, are alive and well in the 20th century. The Chinese people chart their history in an unbroken line back through the dynasties to the world of the gods Nugua and Fuxi, moving seamlessly from a historical to a mythological time-scale.

ANCIENT RELIGION
The earliest archeological evidence supports the existence of the Shang people in the 12th century B.C. in the basin of the Yellow River, "the cradle of Chinese civilization," at about

the same time as the beginning of Greek culture. As in Greece, by the 4th century B.C., China had a society that was highly developed, and many of the distinguishing features of Chinese life then have been passed down in recognizable form to the 20th century. The achievement of such striking stability in their social system is one of the Chinese people's most remarkable accomplishments.

The most important means that China used

Above: A ceremonial ax-head in bronze dating from the Shang dynasty (c. 1500–1066 B.C.). Bronze casting in Shang China was highly developed, both in technique and in terms of decoration.

to secure the survival of its social system was its ability to modify and absorb foreign influences. Those who tried to conquer found themselves in confrontation with a society more complex and sophisticated than their own, and, even when successful in their military endeavor, usually ended by adopting Chinese practices and political structures. This

was the case when the nomadic Manchu tribes conquered China from the north and established the Qing dynasty in the 17th century. But the most significant influence on Chinese development to come from outside its boundaries (that is, until the 20th century and the introduction of Marxism-Leninism) was not brought by invaders: Buddhism was introduced to China by traders traveling the Silk Road from India and Central Asia during the 1st century B.C.

Two religions, or, more accurately, schools of thought, were already well established by this time: Confucianism and Taoism.

CONFUCIANISM

Confucianism is named after its founder Kongfuzi, or Master Kong, who lived between 551 and 479 B.C., during a period known as the "Warring States." After a lifetime spent trying in vain to persuade various nobles and rulers of small states to adopt his ideas on ethics and morals, Confucius died without ever seeing his theories put into practice. His thoughts were collected by his disciples and published posthumously, although it was not until the time of the Han dynasty (206 B.C.–220 A.D.) that Confucianism became the dominant ideology of the Chinese state.

When China was finally unified in the 2nd century B.C., it was really only the Confucians who understood how successfully to run the government and public affairs. Inevitably, they became the senior public figures and civil servants, and Confucian philosophy became more widely disseminated.

Confucius, who was a contemporary of Buddha in India, argued for a highly structured, hierarchical organization of society in which the family was the mainstay of social cohesion. He advocated a strict code of ethics and stressed the importance of good and just government. He believed that a state of harmony could be achieved if everyone was aware of their responsibilities and carried out duties

Right: A Tibetan painting depicting the fate awaiting sinners after death. Note the gods in heaven at the top of the painting.

appropriate to their position. Preaching the virtues of filial piety and maintaining the veneration of those who had achieved old age ensured that the extended families remained close-knit. Although he was noncommittal about the existence of supernatural beings, sacrifices were a vital part of Confucian vision.

RITUAL

By carrying out ceremonies, each person was confirmed in his place in the wider scheme of things and reminded of his obligations and duties. For the individual, this took the form of ensuring that one's ancestors were happy and well catered for, both in their dotage and in the afterlife; at state level, the emperor made annual sacrifices to Heaven and Earth. Confucius's concern was a pragmatic one – to ensure the smooth running of a stable, well-ordered state. His philosophy cannot really be said to constitute a "religion," as it lacks many of the features by which we identify religions, such as a priesthood.

Later followers tried to make Confucianism evolve into a more mainstream religion by building temples, merging the ancient gods with their own beliefs and finally by deifying Confucius himself (although Confucian scholars were firmly against this). Very few early Confucian writings survive, although the classic book *I Ching* ("The Book of Changes") is said to have been written or compiled by Confucius himself.

Left: The massive Leshan Buddha near Chengdu, Sichuan province, is carved out of a sheer cliff face.

Right: The written character shou *("longevity") is designed to resemble the Taoist diagram of "inner circulation."*

TAOISM

The school of thought known as Taoism came into being at about the same time as Confucianism. One of the earliest Taoist texts is a collection of observations, the *Tao Te Ching* ("The Way and the Power"), probably written by the Taoist sage Laozi, in around the 6th century B.C. While Confucianism was more concerned with ethics and politics, Taoist scholars concentrated on more deeply religious questions. At its most philosophical, Taoism argues that there is a natural order in the world that determines the behavior of all things in existence. Early Taoist thinkers believed in the "oneness" of things, the unity of everything in the universe, and hoped that by studying the world of nature they would discover essential laws.

LAOZI

There is some debate over whether this man actually existed (his alleged birth date is 604 B.C.) and many scholars now believe that the book had nothing to do with him. In any case, he became central to the new religion and was deified partly in order to provide competition with Buddhism when that arrived in the 1st century A.D.

TAO AND SCIENCE

This attention to the spirit of things – particularly naturally-occurring phenomena like water or wind – led Taoists into a systematic investigation that became the beginning of science in China. Later on, Taoism operated on a more popular level; the belief that inanimate objects had their own "spirit" or "god" gave rise to a system of worship designed to propitiate these powers which was far removed from the early Taoist principles. Taoist priests also practiced the art of *fengshui* ("wind and

Opposite: A figure inspired by Fan Zeng.

Left: A sleeping monk.

water"), a method of determining the positioning of buildings so that they did not offend the spirit of the site. Taoism had a great influence on the development of landscape painting in China. Its preoccupations are reflected in the subject matter of the genre – the scholar gazing out from the shelter of a rustic retreat at pine-clad mountains shrouded in mist has been depicted over and over again.

BUDDHISM

Introduced from India in the 1st century A.D., Buddhism had grown so popular by the time of the Tang dynasty (618–906 A.D.) that it was powerful enough to challenge the existing religions' monopoly.

One of the most important contributions that the introduction of Buddhism made to Chinese life was the concept of the transmigration of souls. This belief in cyclical life, the view that souls return to the world in a form determined by their behavior during their previous incarnation, offered some comfort to those who perhaps felt that their present existence left something to be desired. The mythology of Hell owes most to Buddhism: on arriving in the Underworld, the soul comes before Yen Wang, the God of Death, who examines the register recording all good and evil deeds. For example, filial sons or believers are able to proceed directly to join the Buddha himself, to go to Mount Kunlun, the home of the immortals, or to be reborn immediately as a human being. Sinners are required to come before one of nine judges who mete out the punishment appropriate to the offenses committed. The taking of life was regarded as the most heinous of Buddhist sins, and it brought about a new respect for living things: vegetarianism became popular as a result of Buddhist influence.

FROM PHILOSOPHY TO RELIGION

Virtually every culture in the world has developed a mythology that revolved around powerful deities, so it is no surprise that the Chinese should adapt each of their philosophical systems in the same way. Such beliefs provide people with an explanation for the world around them, for the unpredictable and mighty forces of nature which can change their lives seemingly at a whim.

Confucianism and Taoism were easily adopted by the nobility and the emperors, who already practised an elaborate form of ancestor worship. But the peasants were largely excluded from these rituals. They placed their faith in sorcerers who claimed to be able to placate evil spirits, and their beliefs were far more similar to the very primitive animist beliefs of the land. Buddhism was clearly far more accessible to the common people, although the faith was adapted slightly to emphasize the importance of the family over the individual.

A PRAGMATIC FAITH

Chinese myths reflect the universal admiration for hard work and bravery. Strangely, for such a hierarchical society, there are also a number of legends in which poor people triumph over dictatorial rulers, showing an admiration for fair play and justice.

The adage "Confucian in office, Taoist in

每汝錯猜卦
人向天下畫裏魅
一九七〇年
於

Opposite: An apsara, *a Heavenly being in the form of a musician flying on a cloud. This 6th-century carving is in the Buddhist cave temples at Longmen, Henan province.*

Left: Chung K'uei, a figure from Chinese legend. He wears traditional costume and is always depicted in the same hat and pigtails.

retirement, and Buddhist as death draws near" sums up the pragmatic Chinese approach to religion. If we aim to rationalize and explain, to codify and authenticate these tales, then we will be exasperated and confounded by the tangled knot that is Chinese mythology. If, on the other hand, we can accept them as meaningful and vivid accounts of a way of experiencing the world, of drawing inspiration and comfort, then we enter a realm that will entrance and delight us.

China is an extremely large country, which has proved itself able to accommodate a vast range of beliefs, and has merged the three main philosophies into something resembling a national religion.

CHINESE LITERATURE

Although China has a long written history, there are many difficulties for the student of mythology. As in the case of the *Journey to the West*, many texts are not as old as they purport to be, with material selectively incorporated by their authors in order to give credence to their own accounts. Often, the same basic myth exists in a number of variations, and there is no one single, authorized version. The *Shanhaijing*, the "Mountain and Seas Classic,' edited in the 1st century B.C., and the *Huainanzi,* the writings of Master Huai Nan, compiled in the 2nd century B.C., are both rich

Above: A Buddhist monastery in the Tibetan city of Lhasa. Tibet was invaded by the Communist Chinese in 1950 and its traditional religious institutions were banned under Chinese rule.

sources of classical myths. During the Tang dynasty, one of the most artistically creative periods of Chinese history, there was much interest in magic and the supernatural, and themes from early myth and folklore were woven into stories written at this time.

CULTURAL TRADITIONS

Confucianism, Taoism, and Buddhism have combined to build up an amazing mythological heritage. Although the Han Chinese constitute 94 percent of the 1 billion population of the People's Republic today, they make up only one of an estimated 50 ethno-linguistic

groupings within China's boundaries.

A DIVERSE HERITAGE

This diverse heritage has given rise to a body of stories that is a rich and vital part of Chinese life. It is impossible to make sense of Chinese literature without a knowledge of its myths, for they are constantly referred to. Today these tales are still the subject of numerous retellings – in book and comic form, or as plays, operas or even movies. In festivals and holidays, in painting and sculpture, as figures of speech, the myths of ancient China live on in the lives of ordinary Chinese people everywhere.

CREATION MYTHS

There are several creation myths in Chinese legend, although the most important is that of the giant Pangu, who emerges from a primordial egg. The egg is a common symbol of fertility, closely connected with creation and birth by many peoples. South Korean legend, for example, tells of an egg that contained a baby who grew up to be leader of the world, and Indian mythology also incorporates a cosmic egg. The concept of a single progenitor of the human race can be found in cultures as diverse as those of Greece and Polynesia. Similarly, the incestuous marriage of Nugua and her brother Fuxi has its counterpart in the Japanese myth of the union of Izanami and Izanagi, a tale which was almost certainly borrowed from the Chinese. The tale of Pangu dates from the 4th century A.D., although its origins may be far more ancient.

Even within China, themes and motifs occur in numerous guises. A folk tale recorded in Hebei province gives Pangu as the maker of the mud figures that became the first humans. And in another story, the union of Tianlong and Diya, attendants of Wenchang, the God of Literature, gives rise to the first humans. The universality of these motifs indicates the similarity of concerns of people the world over; they underline Carl Jung's theories of the "collective unconscious" and the degree to which there is a shared human experience.

Previous page: A porcelain dish decorated with the yin/yang symbol and surrounded by eight trigrams used in divination. Fuxi, brother of Nugua, is usually credited with their discovery.

Left: A vase dating from the 5th to 6th centuries A.D. decorated with the animals that represent the 12 months of the year.

CLASSICAL CHINESE COSMOGRAPHY

The structure of the classical Chinese world is indicated in several sources, and from these it is possible to see that there was a number of cosmographies (theories of the universe). Of the Suan Ye school, very little is known, save that its followers believed the Sun and stars moved freely about the heavens. One school held that the universe was in the form of an egg, in which the sky was painted inside the upper part of the shell and the Earth floated on the ocean that lay in the lower part of the eggshell. A still older tradition, the Zhou Bei school, held that the sky was an inverted bowl rotating around the axis of the Pole Star; the Earth was a square underneath the sky, bordered on each side by one of the four seas. The sky was conceived as a solid dome, supported by four or eight pillars or mountains. The fact that the Pole Star does not occupy a central position in the firmament is ingeniously accounted for in the myth of Gonggong's defeat (see page 23).

A scientifically advanced civilization, the Chinese had a sophisticated understanding of the universe, and some scholars believe that as early as the 1st century A.D. they had calculated that the world must be round.

THE GIANT PANGU

At the beginning of time there was only dark Chaos in the universe. Into this darkness – which took the form of an egg – Pangu, the first living creature, was born. Pangu slept, nurtured safely inside the egg. After many years, when he had grown into a giant, Pangu

Right: Xiwangmu, the Queen Mother of the West, rides on a deer holding a peach and a fungus, both symbols of long life. This is a 17th-century soapstone carving.

Right: Taoist sages examining a painting of the yin/yang symbol. (Detail of a porcelain dish, Kangxi period, Quing dynasty.)

awoke and stretched, thereby shattering the egg. The lighter, purer parts of the egg rose up to become the sky; the heavier, impure parts sank down to become the Earth. This was the beginning of the forces of yin and yang.

YIN AND YANG

The female element, yin, is associated with cold and darkness, the Moon and the Earth; the male element, yang, with light and warmth, the Sun and the heavens. (These ancient Chinese concepts of yin and yang have become familiar to westerners through the popularity of the *I Ching*, or "Book of Changes.")

These two interacting forces balance and sustain the Chinese cosmos; if their balance is disturbed, disaster will befall the human race. The ancient Chinese regarded Heaven as the source of the weather which governed their lives, and knew that sacrifices must be made to the realm of Shang Ti by the Earthly ruler, the Son of Heaven. Just as the yin and yang of the cosmos had to remain in harmony, so the interaction of humans and nature was important to the survival and prosperity of humankind. Humans therefore had to learn to react correctly to the whims of nature.

PANGU AND THE CREATION

Pangu feared that Heaven and Earth might merge together again, so he placed himself between them, his head supporting the sky and his feet pressing down on the Earth. For the next 18,000 years Pangu grew at a rate of 10 feet a day, increasing the distance between the two by the same amount. Eventually both Heaven and Earth seemed securely fixed at a

gap of 30,000 miles, and Pangu fell into an exhausted sleep from which he never awoke.

THE DEATH OF PANGU
On his death, the different parts of his body were transformed into the natural elements: his breath became the wind and clouds; his voice turned into thunder and lightning; his left eye became the Sun and his right the Moon; his four limbs and trunk turned into the cardinal directions and the mountains; his blood formed the rivers and his veins the roads and paths; his flesh became trees and soil; the hair on his head became the stars in Heaven; and the skin and hairs on his body turned into grass and flowers; metals and stones were formed from his teeth and bones, and dew from his sweat. And the various parasites on his body became the different peoples of the human race. Thus was the universe created by the giant Pangu.

There are a number of versions of this myth – although broadly similar, they differ in detail about the eventual outcome of the parts of Pangu's body. Pangu is also sometimes credited with the power to control the weather, the outlook changing according to his temper.

The myth of Pangu was probably added to the Taoist cosmology in the 4th century A.D., as it is an excellent illustration of the yin-and-yang theory.

It is interesting to note the comparatively lowly position accorded the human race. Humans are far from the center of the universe; instead they are small and rather insignificant beings which are simply part of the natural order of creation. Chinese landscape painting reflects this view of the world. Tiny figures appear on great seeping vistas of mountains, lakes, and waterfalls, people being dwarfed by the beauty of the natural world.

Another account of the origin of the human race is given in the following story.

NUGUA PEOPLES THE WORLD
There was once a goddess who was half-human and half-snake (some say half-dragon). She had the ability to change shape and could do so many times a day.

One day, as she wandered through this newly created world, she felt that although there were many wondrous and beautiful things in it, it was a lonely place. Nugua yearned for the company of beings like herself, with whom she could talk and laugh. She came to a river and sat down on the bank, gazing at her reflection in the water. As she mused, she trailed her hand in the water and scooped up some mud from the riverbed. She kneaded the clay into a little figure, only instead of giving it the tail of a snake, like the one she had herself, she fashioned legs so that it could stand upright.

THE FIRST HUMANS
When this little creature was placed on the ground, it at once came to life, prancing around her and laughing with joy. Nugua was very pleased with her handiwork and determined to populate the whole world with these delightful little people. She worked all that day until nightfall, and started at dawn again the next day. But Nugua soon realized that the task she had set herself was immense, and that she would be exhausted before she had made enough people to fill the world. However, by using her supernatural powers, Nugua found she could achieve her wish. She took a length of vine, dipped it in the mud and then whirled it round in the air. The drops of mud that flew off the vine were transformed into little people when they touched the ground. Some say that those who had been formed by Nugua

Right: Court robes from the Qing era (17th century) were embroidered with dragons, the principal symbols of good fortune and royal authori-ty. Yellow was a color reserved for the highest stratas of society.

herself became the rich and fortunate people of the Earth, and those formed from the drops of mud became the ordinary, humble folk. Nugua realized that in order to save the human race from becoming extinct when her original people died, they would need a means of reproducing. So she divided the humans into male and female so that they could produce future generations without her assistance.

NUGUA AND FIXI

Another story recounts that long ago there were only two people in the world: Nugua and her brother Fuxi. They wanted to marry and produce children, but were afraid to consummate an incestuous marriage without authority from Heaven. One day they climbed the sacred Mount Kunlun in the west, and each built a bonfire. The smoke from the two fires mingled together and they took this as a sign that they should indeed become husband and wife. Out of modesty, Nugua made herself a fan of straw and with this she covered her face when they were joined together; it is still the custom today for a bride to hold a fan.

GONGGONG'S DEFEAT

One day Gonggong, the God of Water, and Zhurong, the God of Fire, decided to do battle in order to find out which was the most powerful. After many days of fierce fighting, in the course of which they tumbled right out of the heavens, Gonggong was defeated. He was so ashamed that he resolved to kill himself by running against Mount Buzhou, one of the mountains holding up the sky. The mountain came off much worse from this encounter, as a great part of it came crashing down. A jagged hole was torn in the sky, and great crevasses appeared in the Earth. From these massive chasms fire and water spewed forth,

causing a great flood covering the surface of the Earth. Those who escaped drowning saw their crops and homes consumed by flames.

NUGUA SAVES THE WORLD

Nugua, who had given these people life, could not bear to see them suffer so, and quickly acted to restore order. She chose a number of

Above: A folk papercut depicting the ox-herd in the legend of the parted lovers. He is carrying his two children in baskets suspended from a pole while on his way to visit his wife in Heaven.

These pages: This selection of timeless Chinese figures illustrates the traditional agricultural roots of Chinese religion. They also emphasize the contemplative nature of belief, and show how this had a profound impact on the style of Chinese art.

colored pebbles from the river bed and melted them down into a viscous substance with which she was able to repair the damage caused to the firmament. In order to be sure that the sky did not collapse again, Nugua slaughtered a giant tortoise and cut off its legs. These she placed at the four points of the compass as extra supports for the heavens. Nugua thus restored order to the world and enabled human beings to carry on their affairs in peace.

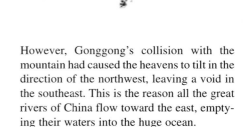

However, Gonggong's collision with the mountain had caused the heavens to tilt in the direction of the northwest, leaving a void in the southeast. This is the reason all the great rivers of China flow toward the east, emptying their waters into the huge ocean.

There are a number of popular and well-known myths concerning the heavens. They reflect an ancient Chinese curiosity in astronomy and the movements of the planets

THE PARTED LOVERS

This legend revolves around an oxherd and a weaving girl, who respectively represent the

stars Altair and Vega, on either side of the Milky
Way. This story holds particular significance
for parted lovers; indeed, a husband and wife
who have been assigned to work in different
parts of the country are referred to in such
mythologically related terms.

A poor young peasant lad just managed to
make a living from his barren soil with the
help of his most valued possession, his ox.
He was honest, worked hard, and was liked
and respected by all, but the young man felt

that his life was empty without a wife and
family. One day his ox revealed to his owner
that he was in fact the Ox Star, sent to Earth
as a punishment for wrongdoing. "As you have
treated me kindly, I will reward you by help-
ing you to find a wife."

THE HEAVENLY MAIDENS

The Ox Star told the young man to go the next
day and hide himself in the undergrowth surrounding a nearby pool, which he said was
used by the Heavenly Maidens to bathe in.
Following his instructions, the oxherd hid by
the pool of clear water, and sure enough, a
group of beautiful young girls soon arrived at
the water's edge. They left their bright clothes
on the bank and stepped into the water. While
the girls were occupied with their toilette, the

oxherd mischievously hid the pile of clothes that was nearest him.

As the girls emerged from the water, the young man came out from his hiding place, causing the girls to panic and, grabbing their clothes, they flew off into the sky. One could not find her garments and was trapped on the ground, terrified. But when the young man spoke to her kindly, she realized he meant her no harm and agreed to be his wife. After their marriage, she divulged that she was in fact the granddaughter of Heaven and the Goddess of Weaving. Thanks to the wife's skills, their fortunes prospered and the young couple were very happy together, a happiness increased still further when they produced two children, a boy and a girl.

THE GODS' DISPLEASURE
But the gods were not pleased at the thought of the weaving maid remaining on Earth, and sent down messengers to snatch her back to her rightful abode. The oxherd and his children watched helplessly as the weaving maid was carried, weeping, back to Heaven. The old ox came once more to the aid of his master: "I shall die soon and, when I do, you must take my skin and wrap yourself in it, then you will be able to pursue your wife." The oxherd did as he was told, and then, placing his children in two baskets suspended from a carrying pole across his shoulders, he set off.

THE GODS RELENT
The oxherd soon caught sight of his wife, but

Left: A New Year print dating from the 17th century of the kitchen god, Tsao Chun. Every home had a shrine to this important deity, who was believed to travel back to Heaven every year to report on the mortals.

before he could reach her he was spotted by her grandfather or, others believe, her grandmother, Xiwangmu, the Queen Mother of the West. A line drawn in the sky became a raging torrent, running between them. The little girl urged her father to use the ladle he had placed in the basket with her as ballast to empty the water from the river. The sight of the devoted family at their hopeless task touched the hearts of the gods, and it was decided that the family could be united once a year. On the seventh day of the seventh month, all the magpies fly up from Earth and form a bridge across the river, enabling the oxherd to cross over and visit his wife. Some say that when rain falls on this day, it is the tears of the weaving maid as she weeps tears of joy.

THE WEAVING MAID'S FESTIVAL

The festival that is held on this date is the annual feast of young girls, in which they entreat the weaving goddess to give them skills in spinning, weaving, and embroidery. It is said that the ladies of the Tang emperor Xuan Zong would shut a spider into a box on this night, and take the web found the following day to be an indication of the skill of the one who imprisoned it.

YI, THE HERO

This legend is rather similar to the European tale of William Tell. Yi was a highly skilled bowman and was known as "the excellent archer." In the time of King Yao ten Suns appeared in the sky, scorching and burning the Earth with their heat, drying up rivers, and destroying crops and plants. The people

Right: Part of a large, traditional figure-painting scroll by Zhu Zhen Sheng showing a scholar and his servant.

began to starve, and centaurs, wild boars, huge serpents, and other monsters began to roam.

The hero Yi appeared and shot down nine of the Suns with his magic bow, restoring order, fertility, and harmony to the world.

This myth reflects a wider interest in, and concern for, knowledge about space and astronomy. As long ago as 200 A.D., the Hsuan Yeh , or "infinite empty space school," argued that "the Heavens were empty and void of substance . . . The Sun, the Moon, and the company of stars float in the empty space, moving or standing still. All are [made of] condensed vapor."

Observation of heavenly movements was a serious and secretive business, and there are records of sun-spot activity dating from the year 28 A.D. The emperors fostered this work, uniting astronomers with sorcerers, engineers, and astrologers in an attempt to exploit the predictive nature of the stars.

DRAGONS

Dragons feature heavily in Chinese folklore, and are totally unlike the evil, fire-breathing creations of European myth. Charismatic creatures, the Chinese dragon, or *lung,* is the rain-bringer, the lord of all the waters, and is now regarded as a symbol of good fortune. Great snaking dragons play an important part in the New Year celebrations.

Ancient inscriptions have been found, imploring the *lung* to revive the Earth with rain. The *lung* were regarded as powerful supernatural beings, able to change shape, altering in size from a silkworm to a creature that could overshadow the whole world. They are composite creatures with the horns of a stag, the head of a camel, the eyes of a demon, the neck of a snake, the scales of a fish, the claws of an eagle, the feet of a tiger, the ears of a bull,

Left: Traditional designs for makeup used in the Chinese theater, each one for a specific type of character.

Above: A page from a contemporary story-book telling the popular legend of the immortal monkey.

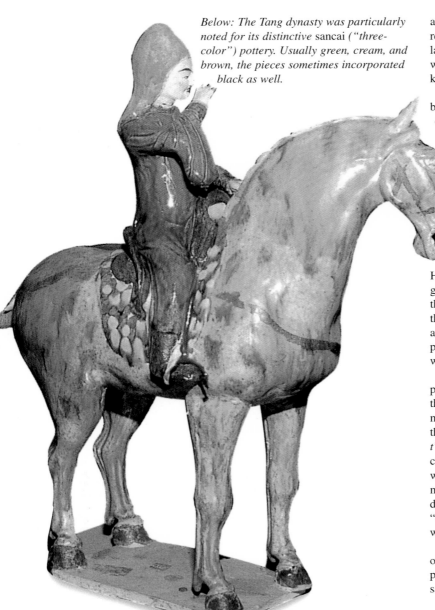

Below: The Tang dynasty was particularly noted for its distinctive sancai *("three-color") pottery. Usually green, cream, and brown, the pieces sometimes incorporated black as well.*

and the whiskers of a cat. Dragons were also regarded as wise creatures, and it was popularly supposed that each one had a "pearl of wisdom" in his mouth. Scholars and sages were known as "dragon men."

It is not surprising that such powerful beasts became inextricably linked with the Chinese emperors, and the five-clawed *lung* was, for many years, the imperial symbol. The Heavenly dragon represents the power of Heaven and thus the yang force at its most potent.

IMMORTALITY

Despite its advocacy of respect and its admiration for hard work, Chinese thought lacks a really clear distinction between good and evil. Humans were regarded as bodies joined together by two souls: the *hun* soul came from the sky and returned to it, and the *pho* from the Earth, where it returned after death. The ancient Chinese believed in elixirs which could prolong life, and Ko Hung, the alchemical writer of the 3rd century, wrote about two.

One restricted the flight of the *hun*, the other prevented the *pho's* return to Earth, allowing the body to roam either the heavens, or in the mountains and forests. Those who "raised themselves up into the airy void" were called *t'ien hsien,* or "celestial immortals"; those who chose to restrict their activities to the Earth were known as the *ti hsien*, the "terrestrial immortals." A third group could apparently abandon their bodies after death, and were thus "corpse-free immortals," although Ko Hung was unclear about where they lived.

Legend has it that Ko Hung prepared pills of immortality and fed one to his dog, which promptly died. He took one himself, with the same result, but while his funeral was being

Left: K'uei-hsing, the much revered God of Examinations, is shown standing on the head of a turtle in this c. 17th-century Chinese figurine. He wields a brush which he will use for recording lists of the successful entrants.

Below: Emperor K'hang-hsi (1662–1722), one of the first Manchu emperors. His imperial robes are covered in dragons, an ancient symbol of his power and authority.

planned, both he and the dog were miraculously revived. Chang Tao-ling, the first Heavenly teacher of the Taoist school, is said to have lived for 122 years after consuming the elixir.

In Taoist belief, the *hsien* roam the universe, and their actions and miracles have produced a rich mythology. The Taoist trinity is called the *San Ch'ing,* or "Three Purities," who are all *t'ien hsien.*

The first is Yuan-shih, the son of the creator Pangu and T'ai-yuan, the holy woman. Able to walk and talk at birth, Yuan-shih was surrounded by a cloud of five colors.

The second immortal was associated with Wu-wang, a member of the nobility who overthrew the tyrant Chou Hsin, the last Shang king, in 1027 B.C. As the *hsien* Ta-chun, he is credited with the establishment of just rule.

The third member of the trinity is the original Taoist philosopher Laozi.

Above: Mythical beasts on the eaves of buildings in the Forbidden City, Peking. These ferocious animals were supposed to frighten away harmful ghosts and spirits.

In order to become a *hsien,* an elaborate funeral was vital, and various rituals were established which would preserve the deceased from physical corruption. The rich used a great deal of jade in their funeral rites. Those who could not afford to prolong their lives had to make do with appeals to the gods who watched over them.

GODS AND
GODDESSES

Previous page: A Tang dynasty bronze mirror of Chang E under the cassia tree.

There is a huge number of gods and goddesses in the Chinese pantheon, which operates like a giant administrative bureaucracy, and reflects the Chinese nation. Subject to the supreme being, the gods' behavior is assessed every year in a divine appraisal system. Old gods leave and new ones arrive, some of whom start life as mortals. It is interesting to note that virtually all Chinese deities are depicted as human beings. Lesser local gods, collectively called the "gods of walls and ditches," are also revered, and every region has its own, so several gods may perform the same function in different parts of the country. The Chinese version of Hell appeared with the arrival of Buddhism, and was immensely complex, with 18 different Hells attached to ten judicial courts, under the jurisdiction of Yen Wang, the God of Death.

Left: The nobility and royalty were buried with all they might need in the afterlife, including attendants. This piece dates from the Tang dynasty (618–907 A.D.).

Pangu was the creator of the universe and Nugua created the first people from yellow clay. She took a special interest in her mortal creations and saved them after the great flood. Her consort (and her brother in some versions) was Fuxi. Both he and Nugua were often shown with snakes' tails. Zhurong, the God of Fire, appeared on Earth next, along with Gonggong, the God of Water, and predictably war soon broke out between them. Leikung was the immensely ugly thunder god. Blue in color, and endowed with wings and claws, he punished sinners who had committed crimes outside the realm of human jurisdiction, such as indirectly causing a death.

HEAVENLY BUREAUCRACY

Chinese people believed that there was a great deal of communication between Heaven and Earth. In fact, Heaven was generally conceived as reflecting the organization of society below: the emperor, who stood at the head of a vast bureaucracy, had his counterpart above, Shangdi. As on Earth, Shangdi was served by numerous functionaries and officials. The supreme ruler, who was also known simply as Tiandi, or "sky," appears in his Taoist guise as the Jade Emperor. The Jade Emperor had daughters, but no sons, in case they tried to depose him. The Queen Mother of the West, Xiwangmu, was the Jade Emperor's wife, who ensured the gods' everlasting existence by feeding them the peaches of immortality which ripened every 6,000 years.

GREAT EMPEROR OF THE EASTERN PEAK

The Ministry of the Five Sacred Mountains (*Wu Yo*) was controlled by the highly revered god T'ai Shan. The grandson of the Jade Emperor, he is known as the "Great Divine Ruler of the Eastern Peak" and was the Jade Emperor's deputy.

As Lord of the Yellow Springs, he headed an office concerned with all matters of life and death on Earth, and controlled 75 departments, each managed by a minor deity in charge of things like fixing the times of birth and death, and determining the span of life of both humans and animals. This accorded with the Buddhist idea of reincarnation, in which one's soul can be reborn many times in higher or lower forms of human or animal life, depending on one's conduct.

T'ai Shan's daughter, Shengmu, the Princess of Streaked Clouds, is a protector of women and children and attends births. This deity was very popular with women anxious to give birth to a son.

T'ai Shan (which literally means "grand mountain") is also the most revered of the five sacred mountains. Each spring sacrifices were offered there by the emperor and it has become an important center of pilgrimage.

THE HEAVENLY MINISTRIES

Each god was in charge of a department, and

Left: Peaches play an important part in Chinese mythology and are symbolic of long life.

*Above: The Pagoda of the Six Harmonies,
West Lake, Hangzhou. Popular belief holds
that building a pagoda is lucky.*

*Left: An 18th-century soapstone figure of
Shoulao, the star god of longevity,
characterized by his bald head and staff.
He holds a peach containing a crane, both
symbols of long life.*

was responsible to the Jade Emperor.

The most important were the Ministry of
Thunder (*Lei Pu*) and the Heavenly Ministry
of Healing *(Tien I Yuan)*, which were run by
the first three sage emperors of China: Fu Hsi,
Shen Nung, and Huang To.

The Ministry of Fire (*Huo Pu*) was controlled by the former Taoist sage and astral
ruler of Mars, Lo Hsuan. Another former

Taoist, Lu Yo, was in charge of the Ministry of Epidemics.

Other major gods includes the God of the Ramparts, Ch'eng Huang, who watches over towns and cities and whose duties are rather similar to those of a deified magistrate. Wen Chang, the God of Literature, heads a ministry which contains, among others, the ugly God of Examinations. He is rather more popular than his boss, since he determines who will come top in examinations.

Some of the most popular gods are now Shou Hsing, the God of Longevity; Fu Shen, the God of Happiness; and Ts'ai Shen, the God of Wealth. He runs a department of lesser gods, like the Immortal of Commercial Profits.

GODS' ACTIVITIES

Many of the gods lived on Earth and returned to Heaven once a year to report to the Jade Emperor on happenings in the affairs of humans. Popular superstition held that many ordinary household objects had their own guardian spirit, and that they required offerings and sacrifices. Although such practices were generally looked down upon by the educated, the mistresses of most households took the precaution of not causing offense, just in case they should receive a bad report!

THE HEARTH GOD

One of the most important of these deities was the Kitchen, or Hearth, God, Tsao-wang, who sees and hears everything that happens within the family. His annual report to the Jade

Right: Guandi, the God of War, who also epitomized justice. Parties involved in a legal dispute would present their case at a temple dedicated to him.

Emperor determines the amount of good or bad luck allotted to a family for the coming year. A statue or image of this god would be kept in a niche above the stove, and during the course of the year he would keep watch over the comings and goings in the house. At New Year, to ensure that he was in a good temper before his journey back to Heaven, he would be offered a good meal and his lips were smeared with honey so that he could only utter sweet words. Then, to the accompaniment of fire-crackers, the soot-blackened image would be burnt to send it on its way.

Like many other Chinese gods, the Hearth God was thought originally to have been a human being. One story tells that he was a poor mason, in such dire straits that he was no longer able to support his wife. Forced to give her in marriage to another, he took to wandering the countryside, begging. By chance, he came one day to the house where his former wife lived. Overcome with shame, he tried to escape by climbing into the hearth, little realizing that it was alight. After his painful death, he was made into a god.

LEGENDARY GODS

Many of the popular Chinese gods were historical characters with outstanding qualities who were deified after death. One of these was Guandi, the God of War, in whose name numerous temples and shrines were dedicated. Guan Zhong, as he was known in his lifetime, was one of a band of three brigands who lived at the end of the late Han dynasty, a period of great turmoil. The story of his life is recounted in *The Romance of the Three*

Left: A Qing dynasty print of a door god surrounded by gods of wealth, along with other acolytes.

Kingdoms, which was written at the beginning of the Ming dynasty – although it purports to be a contemporary account of events – and it has been the inspiration for many plays and novels since. Guan Zhong first achieved renown for his military prowess, but came to be loved for his great courage and loyalty. Guandi is instantly recognizable, as he is always portrayed with a red face.

BUDDHIST DEITIES

Buddhist gods are not nearly so numerous as those from the main body of Chinese myth, but a few bodhisattvas are still extremely popular. One is Ti-tsang Wang Pu-sa, a bodhisattva who wanders the corridors of Hell saving as many souls as possible by selflessly taking on their suffering.

THE GODDESS OF MERCY

The deity held most dear by the Chinese everywhere is Guan Yin, the goddess of mercy, who was originally the male Buddhist bodhisattva, Avalokitsvara. This saint, whose name translated into Chinese means "one who hears the cries of the world," is also the patron saint of Tibetan Buddhism.

Guan Yin is often portrayed as a Madonna wearing a white veil and with a child in her arms; she is worshiped by those hoping for a child. Fishermen consider her to keep particular watch over those in peril at sea, and she is sometimes identified with Mazu, whose cult has spread out from the coastal regions of

Right: A gilt-bronze statue of a bodhisattva sitting on a lotus leaf. He is a Buddhist deity who stayed in the world in order to save others, instead of achieving Nirvana. This figure dates from the Liao dynasty, 907–1125 A.D.

Left: A woodblock print from an 18th-century edition of the classic Journey to the West *by Wu Cheng'en. Monkey is at the top, the monk Tripitaka to the right, and Pigsy center left.*

southern China. There are not only images of Guan Yin in temples and shrines, but also in homes and public places; her figure has been executed in all manner of media – she is the most revered of all deities in the popular pantheon. The following story indicates the degree of affection she inspires.

THE GIFT OF RICE

In the time when people lived by hunting and gathering, life was very hard and uncertain. When Guan Yin saw how people suffered and often died from starvation, she was moved to help them. She squeezed her breasts so that milk flowed, and with this she filled the ears of the rice plant.

In order to adequately provide for the people, she produced such quantities that her milk became mixed with blood toward the end. This is why there are two kinds of rice – the red and the white.

THE DOG AND RICE

An alternative myth gives a dog the credit for introducing rice. After the great floods had been brought under control by Yu, son of Gun, the people were forced to live by hunting as all the old plants had been washed away.

One day a dog ran out of a waterlogged field and was found to be carrying long ears of rice that had got caught up in his tail. When the seeds were planted in the sodden fields they grew and ripened. The people were delighted, and in gratitude, the first meal after the rice harvest is shared with the dog.

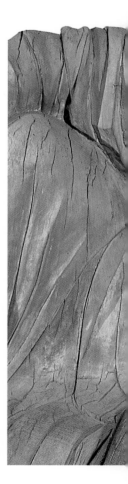

Left: A 14th-century life-sized carved wooden figure of a Buddhist lohan, an enlightened holy man.

THE EIGHT IMMORTALS

The Eight Immortals are central to Taoist mythology. They set an example of ideal behavior so that ordinary people can achieve enlightenment or immortality. Each one was born human and achieved immortality by a different means, such as a selfless act of generosity, through self-denial, or by following a great teacher. They are often shown holding peaches, the age-old Chinese symbol of longevity.

MONKEY

Of all the animals that occur in Chinese myths, both real and fantastic, Monkey is in a class of his own. His story is related in *Xi you ji*, or *The Journey to the West*, written by Wu Cheng'en in the 16th century. This novel purports to be a true account of the travels of the Buddhist monk Xuan Zang, who journeyed to India in the 7th century in search of Buddhist sutras. When he announced that he wanted to return home, his Buddhist hosts were amazed, saying "This is the land where Buddha was born, and if you visit all the holy places connected with him you have sightseeing enough to keep you busy for the rest of your life. Having got here, surely it is a pity to go away!"

But Tripitaka (Xuan Zang is named after the Buddhist scriptures he seeks) explained that Buddhism contained a message for all humankind, so it was his duty to return to China.

After an absence of 16 years, he spent the rest of his life translating the 520 cases of texts that he had brought back with him.

In the book, Tripitaka is accompanied by Monkey and Pigsy, two creatures who, unsurprisingly, have no historical basis in fact whatsoever. Although Monkey has many wonderful supernatural powers, and a sense of mischief and temper to match, Pigsy is a completely down-to-earth character who epitomizes the coarser human desires.

MONKEY'S IMMORTALITY

Monkey was born from a stone egg that had rested on the side of the Aolai Mountain in the Eastern Sea ever since Pangu had created the world. Although in appearance there was nothing to distinguish this monkey from others, he was in fact possessed of magical powers. The tribe of monkeys with whom he lived recognized his special qualities and adopted him as their king. After he had been king for about 300 years, Monkey began to concern himself with the eventual fate that he and his tribe faced. He decided to seek the way of immortality that he had heard of through the tales of the Buddha and other deities. So Monkey left the mountain and traveled to the world of humans. Here he found a master who agreed to take him on as a disciple.

According to custom, Monkey was given a new name – Sun, "the enlightened one," since *sun* is the Chinese word for monkey. After 20

Right: A 16th-century stoneware figure of a judge of Hell. He carries several rolls of records of human souls with their life spans and behavior noted down on them.

years not only had Monkey learnt the secret of eternal life, but he had also acquired other valuable skills, such as the ability to change himself into any form, and fly through the air.

MONKEY'S MAGIC WEAPON

When Monkey returned to Aolai Mountain, he found that a demon monster had taken over the monkeys' home. After defeating the monster in battle, Monkey decided that he needed to get hold of a good magic weapon. He called on the dragon king of the Eastern Sea, and, against the dragon's will, carried off an iron pillar that had been used by the Great Yu, controller of the floods. The size of this pillar could be changed by its owner in an instant, so that it could be made as small as a needle to be carried about and then turned at once into an eight-foot-long fighting staff.

MONKEY AND THE UNDERWORLD

One day, as he was feasting and drinking in the company of his fellow monkeys, Monkey was approached by two messengers from the Underworld, harbingers of his death. When they refused to take heed of his protest that he had become an immortal, Monkey became extremely angry. Laying about him with his magic cudgel, he knocked down his would-be guards, and charged off into the Underworld in a fury. The officials and judges at the courts of Hell were soon beaten into submission by the furious Monkey

He demanded to see the Register of the Dead, and on finding his own entry – "Soul no. 1735, Sun, the enlightened one: 342 years and a peaceful death" – he flew into a further rage. Monkey snatched up a brush and crossed out the lines referring to himself and his tribe. Throwing the book on to the floor, Monkey stormed out, returning to his mountain fortress.

MONKEY GOES TO HEAVEN

However, news of Monkey's exploits began to reach the ears of the great Jade Emperor. Both the dragon king of the Eastern Sea and Yama, Lord of the Underworld, made complaints about Monkey's arrogant behavior. It was decided that it would be a good idea to bring Monkey up to Heaven, where he could be kept under supervision. Monkey was thus offered the post of "Keeper of the Heavenly Horses," and, thinking that this was an important post in the Heavenly bureaucracy, he immediately accepted it.

After a short period in the job, Monkey started to make inquiries about his grade and salary and flew into another terrible rage when he discovered that his was an honorary post that carried no salary and was too lowly to figure in the Heavenly hierarchy. The only way to persuade the proud Monkey to remain in Heaven was to offer him the grand title "Great Sage, Equal of Heaven" (which sounded important but was, in fact, meaningless).

GUARDIAN OF THE GARDEN

After a time, during which Monkey did little but amuse himself feasting and drinking with his friends, he was given the job of Guardian of the Garden of Immortal Peaches in another attempt to keep him out of trouble.

This garden belonged to Xiwangmu, Queen Mother of the West, and, every 6000 years, when the fruit ripened, she would hold a great feast to which the immortals were invited in order to partake of the peaches and renew their

Left: A Qing dynasty porcelain vase decorated in famille rose *enamels. Peaches are credited with the power to ward off evil spirits, as well as being Chinese symbols of immortality.*

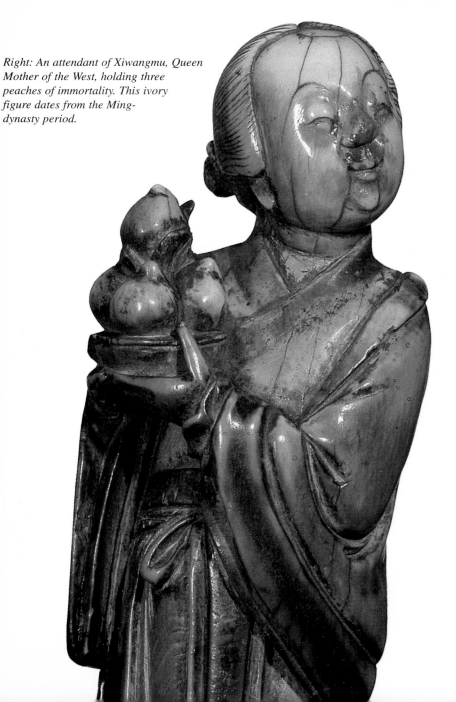

Right: An attendant of Xiwangmu, Queen Mother of the West, holding three peaches of immortality. This ivory figure dates from the Ming-dynasty period.

immortality. It so happened that the peaches were nearly ripe and, of course, Monkey could not resist plucking one to see what it tasted like. It was so delicious that he ate one after another, until eventually he fell asleep in the branches of one of the trees. He was finally awoken by a maid who had been sent to pick the peaches in preparation for the Queen Mother's great banquet.

A SINGULAR FEAST

Monkey was apoplectic when he learnt that he was not to be invited to the celebrations, and determined to seek revenge for being slighted. He had already eaten most of the ripe peaches in the garden, and now proceeded to down great quantities of the fragrant wine that had been prepared for the feast. And when he came across gourds containing the elixir of immortality which Laozi was intending to bring to the occasion, well, he drank that too.

MONKEY'S PUNISHMENT

After a while, when he had sobered up a little, Monkey began to realize the enormity of the offense that he had just committed. Feeling some remorse, he returned to the mountain and hid in his old home. The gods were livid when they discovered what Monkey had done, and determined to punish him.

After many great struggles, Monkey was brought before the Jade Emperor, bound hand and foot. He could not be sentenced to death, simply because he had consumed so many immortality-conferring substances, so it was decided that he should be burnt in Laozi's crucible. But 49 days of white-hot heat gave Monkey nothing more than red-rimmed eyes, and he leapt from the crucible ready to do battle again.

In desperation, the Jade Emperor called on

Buddha himself for help. Buddha was amused by the antics of the insolent Monkey and, placing him in the palm of his giant hand, issued him with a challenge. "If you can leap out of my hand, you can rule over Heaven. If not, you must return to Earth and work to achieve immortality."

Monkey and Buddha

Monkey took a great leap into the air and hurled himself into the distance. When he landed on the ground at last he found himself at the foot of a great mountain. Monkey plucked out one of his hairs and used it as a brush to write his name on the rocks. Then he urinated on the ground, as animals do to mark out their territory, before returning to Buddha. When Monkey claimed his right to be ruler of Heaven, since he had been to the ends of the Earth and back, Buddha burst out laughing.

"You never even left my hand! See, here is your name written on one of my fingers." Monkey saw that there was no way he would ever be able to outwit Buddha, and tried to escape. But Buddha quickly created a mountain and imprisoned Monkey inside it, saying, "There you will stay until you have paid for your sins."

Five hundred years later, after Guanyin's intercession on his behalf, Monkey was released from his prison on the condition that he accompany the monk Tripitaka on his great journey to the West, and protect him from harm.

Right: A papercut image of Monkey about to eat a peach in the Queen Mother's garden. His fur is covered with flowers, coins and swastikas, all symbols of good luck in both India and China. The humor of Journey to the West, *in which Monkey features, has ensured the legend's popularity.*

MONKEY, TRIPITAKA AND PIGSY

The two travelers picked up a third compan-ion, Pigsy, as they continued their dangerous and eventful journey, and after surviving 14 years and 80 perils, the little band finally came within sight of the Buddha's abode, the Mountain of the Soul.

When they had received the scriptures from the Buddha himself, the three set off on their journey home. Thanks to Guan Yin, this time they were able to travel in comfort, riding on a cloud borne by one of the Golden Guardians. This easy lifestyle was brought abruptly to an end when Buddha decided that they should face one more test, bringing the total trials they had undergone to the magic number of 81, nine times nine.

BUDDHA'S TEST

The three companions suddenly found them-selves tumbling down to Earth. On picking themselves up they recognized the spot as being the same bank of a river that they had crossed on their outward journey on the back of a white turtle.

The turtle appeared to ferry them across again, but in midstream inquired whether Tripitaka had indeed found out from the Buddha the lifespan of a turtle, a task that he undertook on their previous meeting. In the excitement of coming before the Buddha,

Left: The Diamond Sutra Scroll is the world's earliest example of a printed book. The frontispiece, which shows Buddha surrounded by his disciples, is dated 868 A.D., and was found at Dunhuang, Gansu province.

Right: A gilded stone carving of the Buddha in central eastern China.

Tripitaka had, in fact, completely forgotten about the turtle's query. On learning this, the turtle was so cross that he promptly tipped them all into the water. Fortunately, they managed to swim to shore with their precious cargo, where they were received with great joy by the local people.

EXONERATION

On reaching the capital, Chang'an, they were brought before the emperor in a majestic ceremony. The three received their final accolade in Heaven, when Buddha announced that Tripitaka was once his disciple, who was sent to Earth in punishment for his sins. Now Tripitaka is to be permitted to take up his place at the Buddha's side again. Monkey is made God of Victorious Battle, and Pigsy is created Chief Heavenly Altar Cleaner.

The story of Monkey has been portrayed in every medium – a books, plays, operas, and movies – and continues to be greatly enjoyed by Chinese audiences. Monkey's mischievous antics and skill at martial arts delight people today, as they have done for centuries past.

Left: The colorful interior of the Hall of Prayer in the Temple of Heaven, Peking.

GREAT LEGENDS

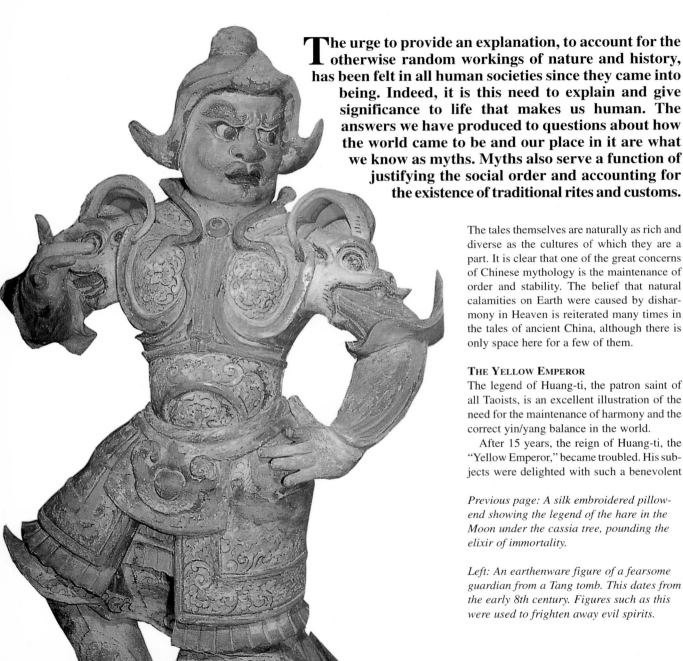

The urge to provide an explanation, to account for the otherwise random workings of nature and history, has been felt in all human societies since they came into being. Indeed, it is this need to explain and give significance to life that makes us human. The answers we have produced to questions about how the world came to be and our place in it are what we know as myths. Myths also serve a function of justifying the social order and accounting for the existence of traditional rites and customs.

The tales themselves are naturally as rich and diverse as the cultures of which they are a part. It is clear that one of the great concerns of Chinese mythology is the maintenance of order and stability. The belief that natural calamities on Earth were caused by disharmony in Heaven is reiterated many times in the tales of ancient China, although there is only space here for a few of them.

THE YELLOW EMPEROR

The legend of Huang-ti, the patron saint of all Taoists, is an excellent illustration of the need for the maintenance of harmony and the correct yin/yang balance in the world.

After 15 years, the reign of Huang-ti, the "Yellow Emperor," became troubled. His subjects were delighted with such a benevolent

Previous page: A silk embroidered pillow-end showing the legend of the hare in the Moon under the cassia tree, pounding the elixir of immortality.

Left: An earthenware figure of a fearsome guardian from a Tang tomb. This dates from the early 8th century. Figures such as this were used to frighten away evil spirits.

emperor, but Huang-ti neglected his imperial duties, passing his days in amusements "till his complexion became sallow ad his dulled senses were stupefied." Another 15 years passed by, causing growing disorder outside his palace, while the emperor himself did absolutely nothing.

He gave up the unequal struggle against the sloth that overwhelmed him and decided to leave all decisions to his ministers. He retreated to a hut in his main courtyard, where he fasted to discipline his mind and body.

One day he dreamed of the kingdom of Hua-hsu, the mother of the great mythical ruler Fu Hsi, a land "beyond reach of ship or chariot or any mortal foot." It was an ideal place, populated by people without desires or cravings, who rode through space "as though walking the solid earth, and slept on the air as though on their beds."

When he woke, Huang-ti announced to his ministers that "The Way Tao" "cannot be sought through the senses. I know it, I have found it, but I cannot tell it to you." During the remainder of his reign, Huang-ti was transformed, and his kingdom assumed an orderliness almost equal to that of the realm of Hua-hsu. On his death, he became a *hsien,* or immortal, and his subjects mourned him for 200 years.

The legend of this astounding emperor is used to illustrate wisdom. His reign has assumed the character of a golden age, and he is endowed with many heroic attributes: slaying terrifying monsters and subduing rebels. His also credited with such inventions as the compass, coined money, and governmental institutions, among others.

THE MOON GODDESS CHANG E
This legend has its roots in the early Chinese fascination with astronomy and the predictive nature of the heavens.

A great mulberry tree called Fusang grew in the sea beyond the Eastern Ocean, and in this tree dwelt ten Suns. These Suns, who were

Above: An intricate, 3rd-century bronze mirror decorated with Taoist deities.

Right: An early 20th-century woodblock print telling the story of Meng Qiang nu. The story begins on the right-hand side, moving top to bottom.

Far right: An elaborate 18th-century porcelain figure of a phoenix, the symbol of the empress of China.

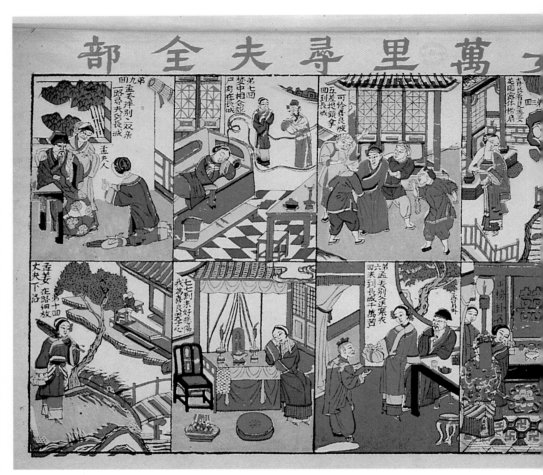

the children of Dijun, God of the East, and Xihe, Goddess of the Sun, took it in turns to go out into the sky. Each morning one of the Suns would be ferried across the sky in a chariot driven by his mother, thus bringing warmth and light to the world. One day, the ten Suns rebelled against the routine and went into the heavens all at once, frolicking across the skies. They enjoyed themselves greatly while they brought disaster down below. The earth dried up, causing all the crops to wither, and even the rocks began to melt. Food became scarce and there was hardly anything to drink. In addition, monsters and wild beasts emerged from the forests in search of prey.

Dijun and Xihe took pity on the suffering of humanity and pleaded with their sons to behave.

YI'S CHALLENGE

In exasperation, Dijun summoned the great archer, Yi, and handed him a quiver of white arrows and a red bow. "I depend on you to restore order on Earth," he said. "Bring my sons under control and slay the wild beasts that are threatening the people." Yi accepted the challenge and set off, accompanied by his young wife, Chang E.

It was clear to Yi that he would get nowhere with threats or persuasion, so he fitted an arrow to his bow and shot it into the sky. A ball of fire exploded, and the air was filled with golden flames. A moment later, there was a thud as something fell to the ground. People rushed forward and discovered that one of their tormentors had been transformed into a three-legged raven. Yi loosed one arrow after another, each reaching straight to the heart of its target. And each time the soul of the Sun fell to the ground in the form of a three-legged raven. The air promptly became cooler and,

but for the quick thinking of the sage king Yao, all might have been extinguished. Realizing that one Sun must remain to provide the Earth with light and warmth, Yao counted the number of arrows in Yi's quiver and made sure that Yi would run out before he could shoot down the last Sun.

With this task accomplished, Yi now turned his attention to the monsters that still threatened the Earth. With great skill and bravery, Yi dispatched one fearsome beast after another, until at last there was peace.

Yi was looked upon as a great hero, and everyone was extremely grateful to him for saving them from a terrible fate. With the sounds of praise still ringing in his ears, Yi returned to Heaven with his wife Chang E to report on his successful mission. But instead of welcoming him with open arms, Yi found that the god Dijun had shunned him.

"Although I cannot deny that you have only done my bidding, I find that I cannot bear to look upon you, you who have killed my sons. You and Chang E must leave Heaven and return to Earth, to those you served so well."

THE EXPULSION OF YI AND CHANG E

Chang E was furious at the injustice of this decision, and felt that it was particularly unfair that she should be punished for her husband's actions. Reluctantly, they packed up their things and moved down to Earth.

Yi was able to fill his days with hunting, but Chang E could find no solace in their new home and mulled over their sorry state endlessly. "Now we have been sent to live in the world of men, and one day, like them, we will die and have to descend to the Underworld. Our only hope is to go to the Queen Mother of the West, who lives on Mount Kunlun, and obtain the elixir of immortality from her." Yi

set off at once, and, after many travails, he at last entered the presence of the Queen Mother. The Queen Mother was moved by Yi's sad story and agreed to help him and Chang E.

THE ELIXIR OF IMMORTALITY

"This box contains enough elixir to give eternal life to two people, although you will still

Above: A glazed earthenware tomb figure of a horse from the Tang dynasty (618–907 A.D.). This is another example of a burial item meant to ease the dead through the afterlife.

Far left: An embroidered pillow showing Chang E on her flight to the Moon.

Right: A 16th- to 17th-century silk tapestry decorated with phoenixes dancing amid peonies and rocks.

have to remain in the world of men. To obtain complete immortality you would need to take twice as much. Guard the box well, for all I have is contained therein."

Yi quickly returned home with the precious box and entrusted it to the care of his wife, planning to wait until an auspicious day to take the drug. But Chang E mused, "Why should I not take the whole amount, and be restored to my former status of goddess. I have been punished quite enough already without justification for it."

CHANG E'S GREED

Immediately after she had taken the elixir, Chang E could feel her feet rise up from the ground. Up and up she began to float, out of the window and through the night air.

"On second thoughts,' she said to herself, "perhaps it would not be such a good idea to return straight to Heaven: for the gods might criticize me for not sharing the elixir of immortality with my husband."

Chang E resolved to go first to the Moon, which was shining overhead in the clear, starlit sky. When she arrived on the Moon, Chang E found it to be a desolate place, empty except for a hare under a cassia tree. But when she tried to move on, Chang E found that her powers had deserted her and she was doomed to keep her lonely vigil to the end of time.

Yi was shocked and saddened when he found that his wife had betrayed him. He took on a pupil, Peng Meng, perhaps hoping that his skills at least would not die with him. Peng Meng studied hard and eventually reached the point where only Yi was better than him at

archery. Peng Meng grew increasingly jealous of his master's superiority, and one day, at an opportune moment, killed him.

WATER IN MYTHS

Throughout the history of China, countless numbers of people have lived alongside the great rivers, the Yangtse and the Yellow River, knowing that the waters that provided them with the means of irrigating their fields could also one day deprive them of their lives and livelihoods. Although the deluge motif occurs in numerous myths the world over, it assumes a particular significance in ancient Chinese mythology. A number of tales illustrate the importance of controlling flood waters, and the degree of respect accorded to those who had such powers.

THE GREAT FLOOD

During the reign of the sage king Yao, Tiandi, the supreme god in Heaven, sent a terrible flood down to Earth to punish humankind for its wickedness. The waters covered the fields and villages, and people were forced to seek refuge in the mountains. They had to compete with wild animals for food and shelter, and their suffering was very great. Of all the gods in Heaven, only one took pity on the plight of those on Earth, and his name was Gun. Gun felt that the punishment meted out was too severe, and pleaded with Tiandi to end the deluge. But his entreaties were in vain.

One day, when he was racking his brains trying to think of a way to control the flood water, Gun came across an owl and a tortoise. When Gun told them of his concern, the owl

Above: Chinese New Year is traditionally celebrated with dragons – symbols of good luck. The dragon is one of the most familiar symbols in Chinese art and folklore.

and the tortoise replied, "Tiandi has a magical substance, which looks just like an ordinary lump of earth. If you could get hold of a piece of this substance and throw it into the water, it would swell up into great barriers that would hold back the flood."

Gun's determination to save the people was so great that he managed to overcome all obstacles and obtained a small piece of the magic soil. He immediately set off for Earth, and dropped a tiny lump into the water. At once, the soil started to heave and shift below the surface, and before long the tips of ridges and mountains could be seen. The flood waters were soon contained by these formations, and then dried up completely. The people were overcome with gratitude for Gun's actions, and danced and sang his praises. But Tiandi was furious when he discovered what Gun had done, and sent the fire god Zhurong down to Earth to seek revenge. Zhurong killed Gun and took what remained of the magic soil back to Heaven, and floods again covered the world.

THE SPIRIT OF GUN

Gun had been killed, but his spirit refused to

die, because he had not accomplished his task. New life began to grow inside his body, which would not decompose. After three years had passed, during which the mourning people had kept watch over the body of their savior, Tiandi sent down a god with a sword to destroy Gun's remains. When the blade slashed at Gun's body, a terrible dragon was released. This dragon was none other than the Great Yu, Gun's son, who took on his father's unfinished mission and eventually brought the flood waters under control. Gun himself then turned into a yellow dragon and went to live at the bottom of the sea.

THE SON OF GUN

Gun's son, the semilegendary emperor Yu, was renowned as a hydraulic engineer. In the *Shu Ching* ("Book of History"), the divine monarch Shun asked him to control the flood waters that still plagued China. Yu spent 13 years "mastering the waters" without once returning home to see his family. He succeeded in taming the waters, so that fields could be irrigated properly, and encouraged schemes of drainage and flood prevention along the Yellow River Valley. He was rewarded by becoming the founder of the first imperial dynasty, the Hsia.

Yu is a Confucian hero, demonstrating exemplary public duty and organizational skills. Taoists, however, believe that his work was a divergence from the natural way of doing things, believing that, to an extent, a human had interfered with nature.

THE SILK TRADE

For centuries, silk and spices were the most valuable trading commodities of the Chinese, and they first began to spin silk as early as 1200 B.C. China is still one of the world's largest

silk-producing nations, and this myth accounts for the origins of silk.

THE LEGEND OF THE SILKWORM GODDESS

There was once a young woman whose father was often away on business, and one day, while grooming her horse she told him how much she missed her father. She announced that she would marry anyone who brought him back to her. On hearing this, the horse immediately bolted off in search of her father.

Many miles away, while in the middle of his work, the father saw the horse, who was neighing at him in an agitated manner. Worried that something had happened to his daughter, the businessmen immediately leapt on the horse and galloped home. On his arrival, he saw that all was well, and asked his daughter why the horse had fetched him. She replied that the horse must have known how much she missed him.

THE DEATH OF THE HORSE

For the next few days, the horse received extra fodder as a reward for his behavior, but the horse appeared unhappy and did not eat it. He only perked up when the daughter was nearby, when he reared up and whinnied in excitement. The businessman asked his daughter why the horse was behaving so strangely, and she remembered the remark that she had made about marrying the person who brought her father home. Having heard this explanation, the man was furious that the horse could presume to marry his daughter. Admirable though the animal was, the man stalked angrily out to the stable and killed him. He

Left: The dragon dance is performed on the New Year. Some regard the dragon as the harbinger of spring and fertility.

skinned the horse and hung the coat out to dry in the sun.

CONSEQUENCES

The next day, while outside with friends, the girl laughed at the skin, but suddenly it flew into the air, wrapped itself around her, and carried her off out of sight. When her father came home, he and the neighbors searched for the girl. They had almost given up hope of finding her alive, when they at last found her at the top of a mulberry tree, wrapped in the horse's skin. She had turned into a strange, wormlike creature, with a horse's head, from which emerged a continuous thread of white silk which she was slowly wrapping around herself.

This is how the girl turned into the silkworm goddess. She later came down from Heaven to present a gift of silk to the Yellow Emperor, who was so pleased with it that he and his wife began to cultivate silkworms, and that was the start of China's silk industry.

THE GREAT WALL OF CHINA

It is not surprising that one of the greatest man-made monuments in the world has acquired a legend of its own. The Great Wall of China was begun during the Qin dynasty, from 214 B.C., to keep out Mongol and Turkish invaders from the north. Some eight feet high, it consists of a brick-faced wall of earth and stone. It stretches 1450 miles, and is a tribute to the engineering skills of the men who built and designed it centuries ago.

Meng Qiang nu's husband was enlisted to help build the Great Wall, an honor of which

his family was extremely proud. After many months, he failed to return, and Meng was very worried. She made numerous offerings to the gods, and asked the relevant authorities about his whereabouts, but no one seemed to have any record of his fate. Finally, it became clear that her husband had perished while constructing the wall – he was just one of many workers whose lives had been sacrificed for the defense of China.

On hearing the news, Meng Qiang nu began to weep uncontrollably. Her grieving did not cease, and her tears eventually caused the wall itself to collapse.

MYTHICAL BEASTS

Dragons are the most important of all the mythical beasts to be found in Chinese tradition. In contrast to western notions, Chinese dragons were believed usually to be well-disposed toward humankind, although subject to rather short tempers! Dragons represent the male, yang element. From the Han dynasty on, the dragon was used as a symbol of the "Son of Heaven," the emperor. The phoenix correspondingly represented the female yin, and the empress – together the dragon and the phoenix are used to indicate a state of marital harmony.

There is a particular affinity between dragons and water in all its natural forms: seas, rivers, lakes, and rain. Four dragon kings were believed to rule over the four seas that surround the Earth, and dragon kings could also be found in lakes and rivers, inhabiting crystal palaces filled with precious treasure. Dragons were held to exercise control over

Left: An earthenware tomb guardian dating from the Tang dynasty.

rainfall, and are often depicted playing with a ball or pearl (the symbol of thunder) among the rain clouds.

NEW YEAR TRADITIONS

At the beginning of the Chinese year, according to the lunar calendar some time in late January or early February, a dragon dance is performed. A line of dancers each hold a stick supporting a section of the dragon's body, from head to tail. A lead dancer holds a lantern in the shape of a red ball. By moving up and down and back and forth, the dancers give the impression that the dragon is writhing around in pursuit of the ball. This dance, which may have originated in an ancient ritual to do with the preparation of the soil before the spring sowing, is performed by Chinese communities throughout the world.

The dragon-boat festival of south China is held on the fifth day of the fifth month of the lunar calendar (around the middle of June). Teams of men in long, narrow boats, with dragon-shaped prows, compete in a rowing race. The loss of a rower overboard was long held to be a sacrifice to the dragon god, and since many Chinese could not swim, this was a not unusual occurrence.

DRAGON LINES

It was widely believed that the landscape was crisscrossed with "dragon lines," veins of the Earth. Before building a house or choosing a

Right: A 17th-century, Ming-dynasty ivory figure of the Taoist immortal Chang Kuo Lao. Traditionally, he traveled on an ass that he could turn into paper. He died while journeying to see the Empress Wu. His body decayed, but he was later seen alive in the mountains.

burial site, people would consult a geomancer to ascertain whether the proposed development was likely to obstruct the natural forces flowing through the dragon lines, thus arousing the dragon's anger and causing calamity. So strong are these beliefs that geomancers are regularly employed, even in somewhere as relentlessly 20th century as Hong Kong. Although officially regarded as pedlars of feudal superstitious nonsense in China today, geomancers continue to advise people, particularly in the countryside.

CHUNG K'UI, THE DEMON SLAYER

During the New Year celebrations, many traditional Chinese homes display pictures of Chung K'ui, the demon slayer, in order to protect their household against demons. Chung K'ui is a popular mythological figure, and there are many legends surrounding him.

One story recounts that he was a poor scholar who passed the state examinations, but was denied a job on account of his extreme ugliness. He committed suicide on the steps of the imperial palace, thereby making the

Far left: The transplanting of rice seedlings is carried out today in the same backbreaking fashion as it has been for centuries; the overwhelming importance of a good harvest informs many of the myths of China.

Below: The Chinese were gifted horsemen, and horses have always featured prominently in their art and sculpture, as in this rubbing from a Han Dynasty tomb decoration

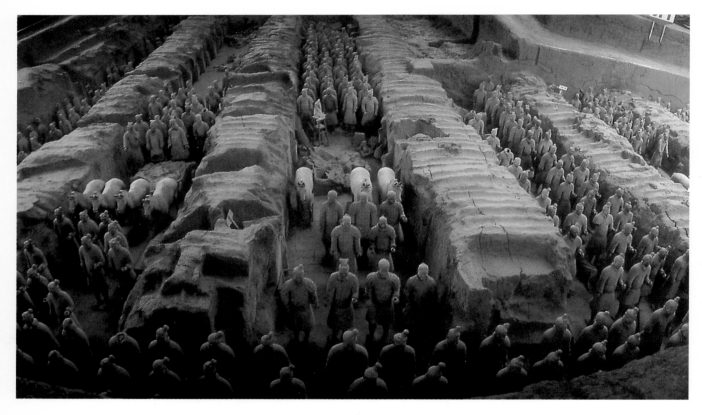

Above: The stately, silent rows of the terra-cotta warriors, life-size stone figures of the Emperor Qin's 3rd-century army.

palace susceptible to demons. The red demon arrived and made the emperor ill, but Chung K'ui's ghost returned and slaughtered the demon with his sword, curing the emperor's malaise. In his gratitude, the emperor gave Chung K'ui a state funeral, and announced that he would henceforth be the demon-slayer of the whole empire. In Hell, Chung K'ui was given control of a sizeable spirit army to help him in his task.

He is often shown riding a tiger (a powerful, *yang* animal) and carrying a demon trap which sucks in the five poisonous animals, the snake, centipede, spider, gecko, and toad. All represent the negative, *yin* element, and in northern China they are expelled on the fifth day of the fifth month.

CONCLUSION

The great Chinese legends reflect a mix of supernatural and practical concerns. They are about harnessing the powerful forces of nature for the good of humankind, as well as being concerned with individual salvation.